WHEN I GROW UP

A Read and Flip Book

By
Charles Mills

Pacific Press Publishing Association
Boise, Idaho
Oshawa, Ontario, Canada

Dedicated to Dorinda,
The beautiful wife
God gave me
When I grew up.

We'll Have a Flower Shop

My sister and I have a secret. Do you want to know what it is? When we grow up, we want to have our very own flower shop.

We both love pretty flowers. In the park near our apartment, there are red flowers, pink flowers, yellow and blue flowers, even purple flowers. Each one is beautiful, and they smell sweet too! We're glad when Dad can take us to see them.

Even though we're sisters, we aren't just the same. One of us likes red flowers the best, and the other likes yellow flowers the best. But we still love each other even though we're different.

In our flower shop, we'll each do different things too. One of us will grow the plants. That's hard work. Flower plants need special care. They have to be watered, protected from bad bugs, and kept warm.

The other one will pick the flowers and put them in a pretty vase. Then she'll show lots of people the colorful flowers. They'll see how beautiful they are. They'll smell the pretty smell. Then, they'll buy them.

We'll tell the people that God made all the flowers in the world. He made them so we'd know that He loves us. I think the people who come to our flower shop will be happy to know how much God loves them.

I'll Be a Businessperson

I live in a big city. Each day, I see many people working very hard, making and selling things like clothes, cars, food, and even toys.

They work in tall buildings and big factories. This is called *business*, and I like it.

Sometimes businesspeople work at computers, typing in letters and numbers, making their company run better.

Some businesspeople travel to other cities, finding places to make or sell their products. They ride on fast airplanes or drive their cars many miles. Last summer, I had my very own business. When I earned money raking leaves, I carefully counted every penny. My dad helped me figure out how much to give to God for tithe—God is my business partner—and then I gave an offering and put the rest of the money in my bank.

I want to learn how to run a business, because when I grow up, I'm going to be a businessperson.

My Dad Is a Businessperson

My dad works in a big city. One day he asked, "Would you like to visit my company?"

I said, "Yes!"

"*BUZZZZZZ.*" The alarm clock woke me up early the next morning. We ate breakfast and then jumped into the car. Soon we arrived

at a tall building. "Here's where I work," Dad said.

First we went to his office, and he made some phone calls. Then we hurried to a meeting. Everyone shared ideas on how to get lots of people to buy products from the company. At lunch we ate in a restaurant with other businessmen and women. And guess what? They talked about business some more.

In the afternoon, we visited offices with computers and fax machines in them. Dad let me make a copy of a letter.

Soon it was time to go home. I waved goodbye to the people in the building, and we drove away. I was tired. So was Dad. Businesspeople work hard every day.

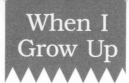

I'll Help Animals

I love animals. I love big ones, little ones, fat ones, skinny ones. I especially love animals that make lots of noise.

I like to take care of animals too. I make sure my little puppy has plenty of food to eat and water to drink. When he doesn't feel very good and can't play with me, I sit and pet him gently and tell him to get well soon. Then I let him sleep.

I think God is happy when we love the animals He created.

When I find an animal that needs some special attention, I bring it home and do my best to make it feel better again. I've helped a bird with a hurt wing, a cat with a cut on its tail, a goldfish, and a big dog that was cold and hungry.

The bird got well and flew away, the cat sat in my lap and purred, the goldfish swam around and around in the fishtank, and the big dog licked me right on the face.

When I grow up, I'm going to be a veterinarian so I can take care of God's wonderful animals and make them happy.

I'll Program Computers

The other day I visited my mom's office. She showed me her desk, her plants, and her pencil sharpener. Then she showed me her computer. I was amazed!

A computer can do all sorts of things. It can help people like my mom write letters, find important information, figure out how much money it costs to do something, and even send a message to a friend in a city far away. And the computer does all this stuff as fast as a sneeze. That's fast!

I asked my mom how the computer knows what to do when you type on it. She said people called computer programmers make the rules for the computer to follow. She said if they didn't make the rules, the computer would just sit there and do nothing.

I looked at the computer and began to think. Maybe I could learn to tell computers how to help people do their business better. I could teach the computer how to help a writer write an exciting story. I could make rules for the computer to follow that would help a teacher explain about animals and nature. Or maybe I could even help the preacher at my church study the Bible for his sermons.

"Mom," I said, "I'm going to be a computer programmer when I grow up so I can help people when they work."

My mom looked at me with a big smile on her face.

"That's a very good idea," she said. "Jesus wants us to be helpful in everything we do."

I'll X-Ray People's Insides

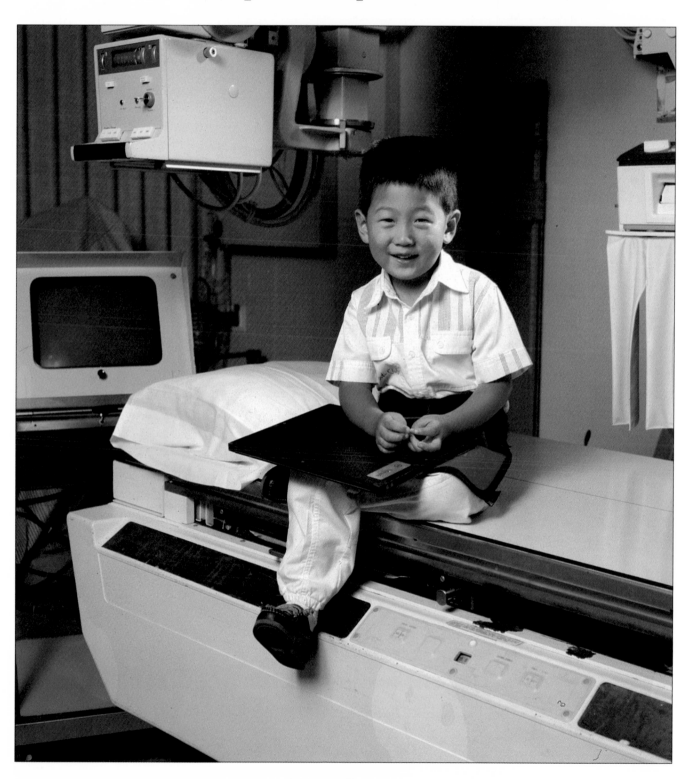

I once fell off my bike and hurt my arm. The doctor said I would have to have an X-ray. I didn't know what that meant.

I found out an X-ray is a picture of what's inside your body taken by a big camera. This camera can see right through your skin and look at your bones. Now that's amazing!

The doctor looked at the picture and said my arm was broken. Well, I could have told him that. It hurt!

Anyway, the doctor fixed me up as good as new. But I got to thinking. That big camera is really a great machine. It didn't hurt me at all, and it showed my doctor something he needed to know about my arm. It's a very *helpful* machine.

The person who takes the pictures with the camera is called an X-ray technician. That's what I want to be when I grow up.

When a boy or girl gets hurt and comes to the hospital, I'll take pictures of their bones to see what the matter is.

The doctor will look at the pictures and then fix the hurting person. I'll help the doctor make that person feel good again.

An X-ray technician works hard to make people happy. Sometimes hurt people are scared. They don't know what's going to happen. The X-ray technician explains about the big camera and how it will help the doctor find out what the matter is. It makes them feel a little better just knowing what's going on.

Jesus doesn't want anyone to be afraid. When you're not afraid, you get well faster.

My Sister Is an X-Ray Technician

 My sister works in a hospital as an X-ray technician. I asked her to tell me what it was like. Here's what she said.

"I usually go to work at eight o'clock and come home at five. But if there's an emergency, I'll go any time the doctor calls.

"First I check the equipment. I want it to operate perfectly for the patients. Then I get busy taking X-ray pictures of people's arms, legs, head, or chest. I smile a lot and tell the people everything will be all right.

"Then I develop the X-rays in a big machine. Soon I carry the pictures up to the doctor's office so he can find out if something is hurt inside the patient.

"Many of the people who work with me are my friends. We help each other when we can't figure something out. We know our job is very important, so we're careful all the time."

We'll Be Farmers

We're brother and sister, and we live on a big farm. Our dad has lived on this farm all his life. Our grandpa grew up here too.

Living on a farm is hard work. Each day you have to feed and milk the cows, take care of the big garden, make sure there are no holes in the fences, keep the barnyard clean, feed the chickens, cut the grass, water the flowers, and do a bunch of little jobs around the house.

Some children might not like living on a farm, but we love it. We get up early in the morning to help Dad out in the barn. By the end of the day, we're very tired and ready to sleep in our comfy beds.

Dad says the best thing about living on a farm is being close to God's nature. It's true. We watch the crops grow tall in the sunshine and listen to the birds singing in the branches high above our head. At night, the stars twinkle brightly in the sky. It's like God lives on the farm with us.

When we grow up, we're going to be *farmers*, just like our dad and grandpa.

We have to go now. It's time to milk the cows.

I'll Make Beautiful Music

I love music. At church, we have a great big organ. I like to listen to the organ while we sing and take up the offering. I especially like it when the organist plays loud. It sounds like many instruments playing at the same time.

My brother can play the trumpet, and my cousin knows how to play the violin.

Not long ago, we went to a band concert. There were lots of instruments—flutes; trombones; bassoons; drums; big, round, shiny cymbals; and a whole lot of trumpets. They played fast songs and slow songs. I liked every one of them!

My favorite music is when people sing or play songs about God. I think God likes to hear them too. It makes me feel like I'm talking to God when I sing a song about Him.

Next year, I'm going to start taking piano lessons. I can hardly wait!

You see, when I grow up, I'm going to be a musician.

I'll Fly a Plane

My favorite place to visit is the airport. I like to watch the airplanes land and take off. They look so beautiful with their broad wings and tall tails. Someday, I'm going to be a pilot. A pilot flies airplanes.

Being a good pilot is hard work. You have to learn about the clouds, the rain, and the wind. You have to know how to fly your airplane to other airports far away and not get lost. And you have to know what to do if something goes wrong when you're in the air.

That's why good pilots are very careful people. They check everything *twice*! You can't stop and fix your airplane when you're flying high above the clouds. You must make sure everything is working right *before* you take off.

Many businesspeople need pilots to fly them from city to city for meetings. Airplanes can carry packages and gifts from one place to another. Some pilots fly over jungles and mountains taking doctors and preachers to help people in faraway countries learn about Jesus.

I'm learning how to be a good pilot right now, even though I'm still little. I take care of my toys, and I'm always careful not to hurt anyone when I'm playing with my friends.

Pilots are very careful people. That helps them get where they want to go. Being careful and safe will help me become a good pilot someday.

Mr. Anderson Is a Pilot

"First you make the propeller spin really fast. Then you race down the runway and zoom up into the sky. It's fun."

That's what Mr. Anderson said. His job is to fly businesspeople to faraway cities in his fast airplane.

"I usually get up early and drive to the airport to make sure my airplane is ready to go. Then my passengers and I climb aboard. The person in the control tower tells me when it's safe to take off.

"We climb high above the clouds and soon land at another airport. Then I wait for the people to come back so I can take them home again.

"While I'm waiting, I check the weather every hour. I want my passengers to get a smooth ride, so I don't want to fly into any storms along the way. When we finally return to our home airport, I put the airplane back in its hangar, ready for tomorrow's adventures."

I'll Help Sick People

Last year, when I was a little girl, I went to the hospital. The doctor took good care of me.

She had some other people helping her. They were called nurses.

Now, I like to pretend that I'm helping someone get well. I make believe that my doll is sick. I listen to her heartbeat, take her temperature with a thermometer, then write some things down on a piece of paper.

My mom pretends that she's the doctor, and we try to figure out how to make my doll well again.

A week ago my doll had a bad cold. She's all better now.

My brother hurt his toe yesterday. I made him go to bed. Then I put two band-aids on his toe. He said it didn't help, but I know it did.

I think God wants me to help people when they're sick. His Son Jesus helped a lot of people get well when He was here on earth.

That's why, when I grow up, I'm going to be a doctor or a nurse.

I'll Print Books

I don't know how to read yet, but I like books. Some books have pretty pictures in them. I look at the pictures while my mom or dad reads to me.

Some books and magazines have stories about animals, interesting boys and girls, and beautiful places to visit.

My very favorite book is about a beaver. When I hear the story, I pretend I'm watching the beaver family swim around on their pond.

I like the many colors in my books too. Some pictures have red and blue in them. Some pictures are yellow and green. My book showed me that beavers are brown and giraffes are tall.

My mom and dad read to me from the Bible. I'm learning about Jesus. I like to pretend I'm sitting on Jesus' lap and He's telling me stories.

When I grow up, I'm going to be a printer so I can make lots of books for people to read that will teach them about Jesus.

I'll Be a Preacher

I like to help people. Whenever I see somebody who is sad, I try to figure out how to help him be happy again.

The pastor at my church says I'm a very good assistant. I always make sure the hymnals are in their racks and there is no paper on the floor.

I like to hear stories from the Bible.

Sometimes at nap-time, I tell my little sister a story so she'll be quiet. She listens to me and smiles. Then she goes to sleep.

When I pray, I pray for *everybody.* I pray for Teresa, my baby-sitter; Mr. Roberts at the grocery store; my friend Barry; my mom; my dad; my sister; Uncle Mike; my grand-mother; even our dog Archibald. My dad says the whole world gets blessed when I pray.

I don't like it when people get mad at each other. God says we're supposed to love each other. I want to tell them that.

When I grow up, I'm going to be a preacher. Then I'll tell everybody how much God loves them. I'll pray for them too.

I'll Be a Plumber

Drip, drip, drip. That's the noise water makes when it's leaking out a pipe under the sink.

Drip, drip, drip. Something needs to be done right away!

Don't worry. Here comes the plumber. When water is leaking, the plumber knows just what to do.

Tap, tap, tap. Squeak, squeak. The plumber moves the pipes around, puts a new connection here and one over there, and tightens everything with a big wrench.

Now listen . . . no more drip, drip, drip. The plumber has fixed the leak!

Water can make floors and ceilings buckle and crack. It can make metal things rust and break. A little water leak can do a lot of damage if it's not fixed right away. Plumbers help people save lots of money by keeping water leaks from damaging expensive things like walls, ceilings, and floors.

Plumbers know little leaks now can cause big problems later. I think Jesus understood that because He said little sins in our lives can cause big problems to come to us later. Plumbers fix little prob-lems before they can get big. That's a good idea, don't you agree?

When I grow up I'm going to be a plumber so I can fix little leaks before they cause big problems. And today, I'm going to work on my little sins too. I'm going to ask Jesus to help me be kind and loving. I don't want to drip, drip, drip.

I'll Write Books

Last night I went to Africa. I saw smiling faces, hard-working farmers digging in the ground, and children playing. I even saw a lion sitting in a tree!

This may surprise you, but I went to Africa in my bed. You probably wonder how I did that.

You see, my mom read me a story about Africa from a book. The story told how beautiful Africa is and how friendly the people are. I closed my eyes and pretended to go to the places the story talked about. It was fun.

When I grow up, I'm going to be a writer. A writer puts exciting stories about people and places in a book. Then other people can enjoy reading about what the writer saw and pretend to go there too.

A writer can also tell people how to do things like paint a house, make a pretty dress, cook a delicious meal, or understand a problem. A writer can tell people about Jesus too. This is the most important thing a writer can do.

The Bible has many writers in it. They tell happy stories and sad stories. Each writer wrote about God and how much He loves us.

I'm going to write books that make people happy. When they read my books, they can close their eyes and see things they've never seen before. If I work very hard and write the very best I can, maybe I can help them see Jesus.

Mrs. Humphrey Is a Writer

 "*Clickity-clack, clickity-clack.*" That's the sound my neighbor, Mrs. Humphrey, makes when she works. She's a writer. Sometimes I visit her home-office. Mrs. Humphrey always stops typing on her computer and talks to me.

"Being a writer means you have to think a lot," she told me. "You spend several hours each day figuring out *what* to write. I like to create books for children to read, so I say to myself, 'What kind of stories do boys and girls like?' Sometimes I go to the library to find out what other people have written. When I get a new idea, I switch on my computer and begin tapping the keys.

"When my book is finished, I send it to a company that promises to print it. They pay me some money, and I start my next book. That's what it's like to be a writer."

I'll Cook Good Food

Yesterday my friend came to visit me. We played cars. At suppertime I said, "If you can stay, I'll show you a surprise."

He called his dad, and he said it was OK.

I went to the kitchen and looked into the refrigerator. I took out the milk, lettuce, and mayonnaise, and a plate of sliced tomatoes and avocados. Then I went to the breadbox and got out a loaf of whole-wheat bread. We had a bag of already popped corn, so I got it out too.

My friend asked, "What are you doing?"

"My mom's busy, so I'm fixing supper," I said.

I put four pieces of bread on a plate and spread a smooth, thin layer of mayonnaise over them. Next I put on tomato and avocado slices, tore off some fresh lettuce, and put another piece of bread on the top. I put each sandwich on a plate.

"You made sandwiches!" my friend said. "And you didn't make a big mess at the same time."

"Of course." I laughed, slowly pouring milk into four tall glasses. "A good cook is very careful. A cook tries to make food look and taste good, and makes it healthy too. Jesus wants us all to be healthy and strong and not hurt our bodies. See, I'm using whole-wheat bread and fresh milk. No candy or soft drinks in *this* kitchen."

My friend nodded. "I'll eat with you any time."

I smiled. Being a careful, thoughtful cook helps people to enjoy eating and to stay healthy at the same time. That's why I want to be a cook when I grow up.

I'll Take Care of Children

When you hear a little baby crying, what do you want to do? Cover your ears? Run away?

When I hear a baby crying, I want to go quickly and see what the problem is. Maybe the baby is hungry. Maybe it needs changing. To me, a baby's cry is just like talking, only a lot louder!

Babies and little children need very special care. They need someone to watch over them, protect them, and love them. That's what mommies and daddies are for.

But sometimes both mommies and daddies have to work hard so they can buy food and clothes for their children. When this happens, they look and look for kind people to help take care of their little boy or girl while they are away earning money at work. These kind people are called day-care operators. That's what I want to be when I grow up.

Day-care operators make sure boys and girls are safe and happy. They give them good, healthy food to eat. They help little babies stay warm and dry.

They talk to the little children and read fun stories from a book. This keeps the boys and girls happy while their mommies and daddies are working.

Jesus loves children very much. I want to be a kind day-care operator just like He would be.

We'll Be Parents

The other day my brother and I were playing with my favorite doll Elizabeth. She was crying, so I held her close and rocked her back and forth in my arms.

"Don't cry, Elizabeth," I said. "I'll take good care of you."

We know Elizabeth isn't a *real* baby, but we like to pretend she is. Ricky makes sure she has delicious play food to eat. I put a warm sweater on her when it's cold and always kiss her good night.

Sometimes Elizabeth doesn't feel good, so I stop whatever I'm doing and hold her close to me. I think this makes her feel better.

When I take good care of Elizabeth, I feel happy inside.

Someday Ricky is going to get married, and I am too. I'm going to have a real baby of my very own to care for. Ricky says he is going to have three babies. We will make sure our children have happy homes to live in.

As they grow, we'll help our children understand how to be helpful and forgiving. We'll want them to know that Jesus loves everyone—boys, girls, mommies, daddies—everyone. Each day we will show our children how to love other people too. That's what parents do.

Parents have a very important job. Moms and dads have to work hard to make sure their children are safe and happy. Boys and girls depend on their parents for *everything*.

If I have a daughter, I think I'll name her Elizabeth. Now why do you think I want to do that?

Our Mom and Dad Are Our Parents

Our parents do many jobs each day. But the one we like best is when they take care of us.

In the morning Mom and Dad rush around getting everybody up, dressed, and fed. Then it's off to school for us, off to work for them. During the summer, we have a sitter who takes care of us until Mom and Dad get home around suppertime.

Mom fixes the meal while Dad mows the lawn. Sometimes Dad fixes the meal and Mom mows the lawn. Just between you and us, we like it best when Dad mows.

On Tuesdays, Mom and Dad sit down and pay the bills. It's not a good time to bother them. Other nights, after homework and chores we play games or read to each other or watch TV together. After family worship, Mom and Dad tuck us into bed and kiss us good night. Being a parent is hard work. But Mom and Dad say we're worth all the effort.

I'll Be a Scientist

I like to learn about animals and flowers. When I go for a walk with my mom, she tells me about nature and about God. She says God created everything in the whole world. I think He did a very good job.

Sometimes I wonder what makes it rain and how birds can fly so high. Yesterday, I sat and watched a bug climb a blade of grass. I think even bugs are beautiful.

In my room, I have a lot of picture books about nature. Before I go to sleep at night, I look at the pictures of colorful rocks and little, tiny animals that you have to look into a microscope to see. I want to know what their names are and find out why God created them.

I guess my questions will be answered someday, because, when I grow up, I want to be a scientist.

I'll Build Houses

I like to build things, which is good because my little brother Matthew likes to knock things down.

One of my favorite toys is my box of wooden blocks. I pretend that I'm making a tall office building or a new shopping mall right in my bedroom.

I very carefully put one block on top of another until my buildings stand strong and tall. Then I build a bridge so my cars and trucks can come across the river for a visit.

When I build something, I have to think about how to make it strong so it won't fall down. Not only do I want my pretend shoppers to feel safe in my new shopping mall, I want to feel that I've done the very best I can.

Then, of course, there's always Matthew.

It's important for me to build things I can be proud of. My kindergarten teacher says Jesus wants us to do our very best in everything we do.

Sometimes my dad looks at something I'm building and says, "I'd like to live in that house. I can see you're being very careful to make sure it's as strong and safe as it can be."

When I grow up, I'm going to be a construction worker and build lots of buildings, maybe even a house for my dad to live in. If I build a house for Matthew, I'll make it extra strong.

25

I'll Take Pictures

I think a camera is a wonderful thing. It helps me remember how something looked even when it has gone away.

My mom takes lots and lots of pictures with her camera. She works for a newspaper, so she has to take pictures of everything that happens in our city.

Last week, she took a picture of me and my friend Carl. We were having fun on the swings in the park.

Now, when I want to remember the fun I had, I just look at the picture. I see Carl and me laughing and playing together. I like to remember things when I look at pictures.

Mom says God made many beautiful things to take pictures of. I like flowers. I want to have a whole bunch of flower pictures hanging on the wall behind my bed. Then, when I look at the pictures, I can remember how much Jesus loves me.

Mom let me take some pictures with her camera. I put them in a little book. I have a picture of my cat, the tree outside my window, my foot, and my mom—she was brushing her teeth.

When I grow up, I'm going to be a photographer and take lots of pictures so other people can enjoy the beautiful things Jesus made.

My Mom Is a Photographer

"Hurry up," my mom calls from the car. "Or we'll miss it."

I jump into the back seat. "Where are we going?" I ask.

Mom steers the car down the street. "I have to take a picture of the mayor of our city. He's giving a speech at a factory nearby."

Mom is always in a hurry. As a photographer, she spends her day looking for pictures to take. Sometimes it's easy. But sometimes she has to grab her camera and race away before the picture is gone.

Last night she had to get out of bed and rush over to the hospital. A woman had three babies all at the same time! Mom said that'll make a great picture-story for the newspaper. Sure enough, there was my mom's photo on the second page of the morning paper.

Photographers keep busy each day making sure everyone can see what happened, no matter what, no matter when, no matter where.

I'll Fix Cars

Cla-tick, cla-tick, cla-tick. Shi-pop, shi-pop. Thump, thump thump. Pssssssssst. Clank!

If your car ever makes those noises, you're in big trouble.

When my mom's car made sounds like that, she had to call a big tow truck to come and get us. I thought it was fun. My mom didn't think so.

A man dressed in dirty clothes looked at the engine of our car. He twisted this, tapped that, pulled on something else. Every once in a while he'd say, "Uh-huh," then, "Mmmmmm."

I watched and watched. He put a shiny round thing over on this side of the engine and put a rubber tube on the other side. Then he poured some green stuff down a hole.

When he was finished, he asked my mom to start the engine. All the clanking, thumping, and shi-popping were gone! The engine went, "*Rorrrrrrrr, rorrrrr.*" Mom smiled. The man in the dirty clothes smiled. And I smiled too, because I had decided something.

When I grow up, I want to be an auto mechanic. That's someone who works on car engines. Then I can help people when their car makes funny noises. I can help them get home safe and sound. People need their cars to get them to work on time, to have fun on vacation, or to just enjoy driving around the country. I know Jesus would be happy for me to fix car engines. He likes it when we help people. And besides, where else can you get really dirty and still make your mom smile?

I'll Fight Fires

A fire can make you warm on a cold winter's night. It can cook your food and give you light to see by.

But a fire can also be very dangerous. If you're not careful with it, a fire can burn your house down. That's very sad.

Near where I live is a fire station. Every time my dad drives by it, I wave. The people who work there wave back at me. They know I want to be a firefighter someday, just like they are.

Firefighters know how to do many things. If a fire starts to burn in someone's house, they jump into their big red or yellow truck and hurry through town. *Rrrrrrr. Rrrrrrr* goes their siren. It's telling all the cars, "Watch out. Watch out! We're coming. Get out of our way. We must stop the fire!"

After they get to the house, they make sure everyone is safe. If someone is hurt, they help them. They turn on the big hoses and spray water on the fire. If the fire isn't too big, they can stop it and save the house from burning down. They also make sure the fire doesn't spread to other houses nearby. It's very hard work.

Firefighters also teach people how to be safe in their homes. They don't want anyone to have a problem with fire. I like that. It reminds me of what Jesus does for us. He wants us all to be safe and happy. But, if there's a problem, He comes quickly to help us.

When I become a firefighter, I'll do like Jesus does. I'll teach people how to be safe and happy. But if something happens, I'll be ready to help.

I'll Talk on the Radio

I love to talk. My dad says I talk more than anyone in the whole world. That must be a lot, because my Uncle Delbert talks in his sleep!

When I talk, I always try to say something important. Like the other day. Mom asked me if it was raining outside. I told her it wasn't raining right now, but, because there was a big bunch of clouds up in the sky and because the wind was blowing harder and harder and because it rained yesterday and the day before, it probably would rain again today, maybe in just a few minutes.

She looked at me and said, "Thank you."

My dad once took me to a radio station.

He said someday I'll probably own one. I listened to people talk and talk. They told the latest news, mentioned which baseball teams had won, said what singer was going to sing a song, and invited everyone to buy food at Martin's Food Store.

The man at the station said many, many people listen to him talk every day.

That's when I decided I want to be a radio announcer when I grow up. Imagine! All those people just waiting to hear what you have to say. I could tell them to be kind to each other. I could tell them to remember to feed their pets. I could tell them that Jesus loves them very much. With just a few words, I could make many people happy. What more can I say?

My Neighbor Is a Radio Announcer

My neighbor has a job at a radio station near our house. But he doesn't go to work during the daytime. He works late at night, when boys and girls like me are sleeping. He says many grown-ups enjoy hearing music even when it's dark outside.

He says he goes to the station and chooses some pretty songs to play. Then he collects news stories from a machine by the door. Finally, when it's time for him to talk, he's ready. "Good evening, everyone," he says. "Welcome to my program. I hope you like the music."

Then he switches on the CD player and makes sure the sound level is just right. Soft, pretty music plays in radios all around the countryside. Radio announcers spend the whole day, or night, playing music and talking to people they can't even see. Neat, huh?

I'll Drive a Truck

Whenever I go on a trip, I like to watch the big trucks driving down the highway. Sometimes they honk their horn for me. Honk, honk. Sometimes the truck driver waves at me. It's a lot of fun.

Those big trucks carry lots and lots of things from city to city. Sometimes they carry shoes, sometimes apples and oranges. I saw a truck that had some cars on it! Those trucks must be very strong to carry such heavy weight.

As I go from place to place with my mom and dad, I look out the window and watch the farms and forests pass by. I see cows and tractors, tall buildings, and big blue lakes. There is always something to see as we ride down the road.

When a truck goes up a steep hill, it makes a big roaring sound. *Rhumm, rhumm!* I like to listen to the truck's engine. *Rhummmm, rhumm!*

When I grow up, I'm going to be a truck driver and drive a big, noisy truck from city to city. When I meet other truck drivers, I'll tell them about Jesus. Then they can think about heaven as they drive down the road. If I see a little boy like me, I'll honk my horn. Honk!

We'll Be Missionaries

In Sabbath School we sing a pretty song. The words say, "Jesus loves me, this I know, for the Bible tells me so."

It makes me very happy to know Jesus loves me. But there are many boys and girls, moms and dads, who don't know that Jesus loves them. They don't go to church. This makes me feel very sad. This makes Jesus sad too.

In the Bible, Jesus says we should go and tell the whole world about His love. That's what I'm going to do when I grow up. I'm going to be a missionary.

Being a missionary is more than telling people about Jesus. It's helping them find good food to eat and clothes to wear. It's giving them medicines so they can get well.

Many people don't even have houses to live in, so missionaries get busy and help them build some. If there's not enough food for everybody, missionaries help the hungry people plant big gardens.

When some people don't have enough clothes to wear, missionaries ask friends and neighbors to bring shirts, pants, and shoes to church. Then a big boat or truck takes these wonderful gifts to the places they are needed most. Missionaries work very hard helping people.

Jesus was the best missionary in the world. He traveled from His home in heaven, helped people find food to eat, healed them when they were sick, and told them how much He loved them. This made many, many people very happy. Making people happy is what missionaries do best.

You don't have to wait until you're grown up. You can tell your friends and family about Jesus today. Why not start being a missionary right now?

MY TALENTS FOR JESUS

A Read and Flip Book

By
Charles Mills

Pacific Press Publishing Association
Boise, Idaho
Oshawa, Ontario, Canada

SBN 0-8163-1115-3

780816 311156

Dedicated to my dad, R. C. Mills,
Who showed me how to use
My talents for Jesus.

Edited by Aileen Andres Sox
Designed by Tim Larson
Photography by Charles Mills
Typeset in 13/16 Bookman

Library of Congress Cataloging-in-Publication Data:

Mills, Charles, 1950-
    [My talents for Jesus]
    My talents for Jesus ; When I grow up / Charles Mills.
        p.   cm.
    Summary: When read from one direction, the book describes how some children use their special abilities, and from the other, it tells different jobs they can do when they grow up.
    ISBN 0-8163-1115-3
    1. Children—Religious life—Juvenile literature. 2. Stewardship, Christian—Juvenile literature. 3. Vocation—Juvenile literature. 4. Vocational guidance—Juvenile literature. 5. Christian life—1960—Juvenile literature. [1. Christian life. 2. Occupations.] I. Mills, Charles, 1950-   When I grow up. 1992. II. Title.
BV4571.2.M55   1992
248.8'2—dc20   92-26393
                                                                    CIP
                                                                    AC

92 93 94 95 96 ● 5 4 3 2 1

I Can Smile

When Jesus made me, He gave me a talent of my very own. Do you know what a talent is? It's something you can *do* that's special.

Some people can sing songs for church. That's a talent. Other people can draw beautiful pictures. That's a talent too.

My mother has a talent. She helps people get well when they're sick. My mother is a doctor. She says she enjoys using her talent every day to make people feel better.

My special talent is on my face. When Mom is tired or sad, I smile at her and say, "I love you." She says it makes her feel happy again. I smile a lot because I like to make my mom happy.

I smile at other people too. Sometimes when my neighbor drives by our house, I smile at him. He waves at me.

When my baby brother Triston starts to cry, I look at him and smile. Sometimes he stops crying and begins to laugh. Sometimes he throws his rattle at me. Smiling doesn't work for everybody.

I'm glad Jesus gave me a special talent. I'm going to use it every day.

Maybe you have a "smile talent" too. Smiling is a talent anyone can have. Why don't you test it to see just how well a smile talent works?

3

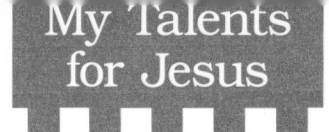

I Know How to Make Friends

Jesus gave me a very special talent. Would you like to know what it is?

Pretend you're new to my town. You come to my classroom, and you don't know *anybody* there!

Then you hear someone say to you, "Hi, my name is Tommy. Would you like to sit over here with me? I can show you how to draw a picture of a horse."

That person is me. My talent is *making friends.*

My teacher always puts new kids beside me because she knows I'll make them feel welcome.

Sometimes a new family will move into our neighborhood. If they have any kids my age, I'll walk right up and say, "Would you like to play space voyage with me?" Usually they do. Other times they're shy and run away. That's OK. Making friends sometimes takes a few days.

My dad told me the secret of making friends. I'll tell it to you so you can find out if you have this talent too. Whenever you see a boy or girl who looks like he or she needs a friend, think to yourself, "What can I do to make that person happy?" When you figure it out, do it.

Jesus was a Friend to everyone. I want to be just like Jesus.

Use Your Talent—Watch It Grow

Write the names of two people you think could use a friend. Then the next time you see one of them, invite him or her to play a game with you. If he refuses, write someone else's name on your list and try again. If she agrees, draw a star by her name.

Start a Friendship Club. Invite anyone who would like to join to come to the meetings. During your get-togethers you can play games, watch videos, share exciting stories, help clean up the neighbor's yard, or learn how to paint pictures. There are many easy ways to have fun when you're with friends.

Find several new pen pals in a faraway place like France, India, South America, or Africa. Ask them to tell you about their home life, school, and hobbies. Try to learn as much as you can. Then share the letters with friends who live near you.

I'm Coordinated

What do pouring a glass of milk, catching a fly ball, and getting an A in handwriting class all have in common? The answer is a special talent from God. You may have it. I know I do. That talent is coordination.

Applying your coordination talent means being careful when you use your arms, legs, hands, and feet.

My friend Tracy doesn't use her coordination talent very often. When she pours a glass of milk, she makes a big mess. Milk goes everywhere!

When I pour myself some milk, I'm very careful not to spill. By being careful, I don't make as many messes.

Baseball is my favorite sport, but I have to work hard to play the game well. I practice and practice. This is helping my coordination talent get better. My feet and hands know what to do when I want to catch a fly ball. Good coordination makes the game exciting.

My handwriting teacher says my letters look very neat. Again, I have to practice so my fingers know how to form the words, but when I'm careful and take it nice and slow, my writing looks pretty good.

Good coordination happens when your body and brain work together. I've found when I take care of my body by eating healthy foods, and when I exercise regularly, my coordination improves. God knew this would happen. That's why He wants us to take care of our minds and bodies. Who wants to make messes all their lives?

I Like to Learn

When I was little, I found out I had a special talent. I like to learn things. I like to look at a book and find out what the pictures mean. At school, I learn what the words mean too.

Each day my teacher brings me more and more things to learn. She tells me about the faraway countries and the people who live there. She lets me draw pictures from a book and then tells me about what I've drawn. Yesterday I drew a picture of an elephant. Did you know elephants make a noise that can be heard by other elephants miles away, that no human can hear? I was surprised when I learned that!

Last year I learned how to add a whole bunch of numbers together. I read a story about a beaver and one about a little boy who lives in a desert. To me, learning is fun!

My mom says learning is a talent. She says Jesus wants us to learn how to read, how to add numbers, and how to be friends with people all over the world. She says we have to learn how to do many things so we can help other people find out about God's love.

Jesus liked to learn things too. When He was a little boy, His mother taught Him about nature and about people. His father taught Him how to work and how to be a carpenter. When He grew up, He used what He had learned to love everyone, even those who hurt Him. Learning to love is the best way to use this very special talent.

My Prayers Can Help

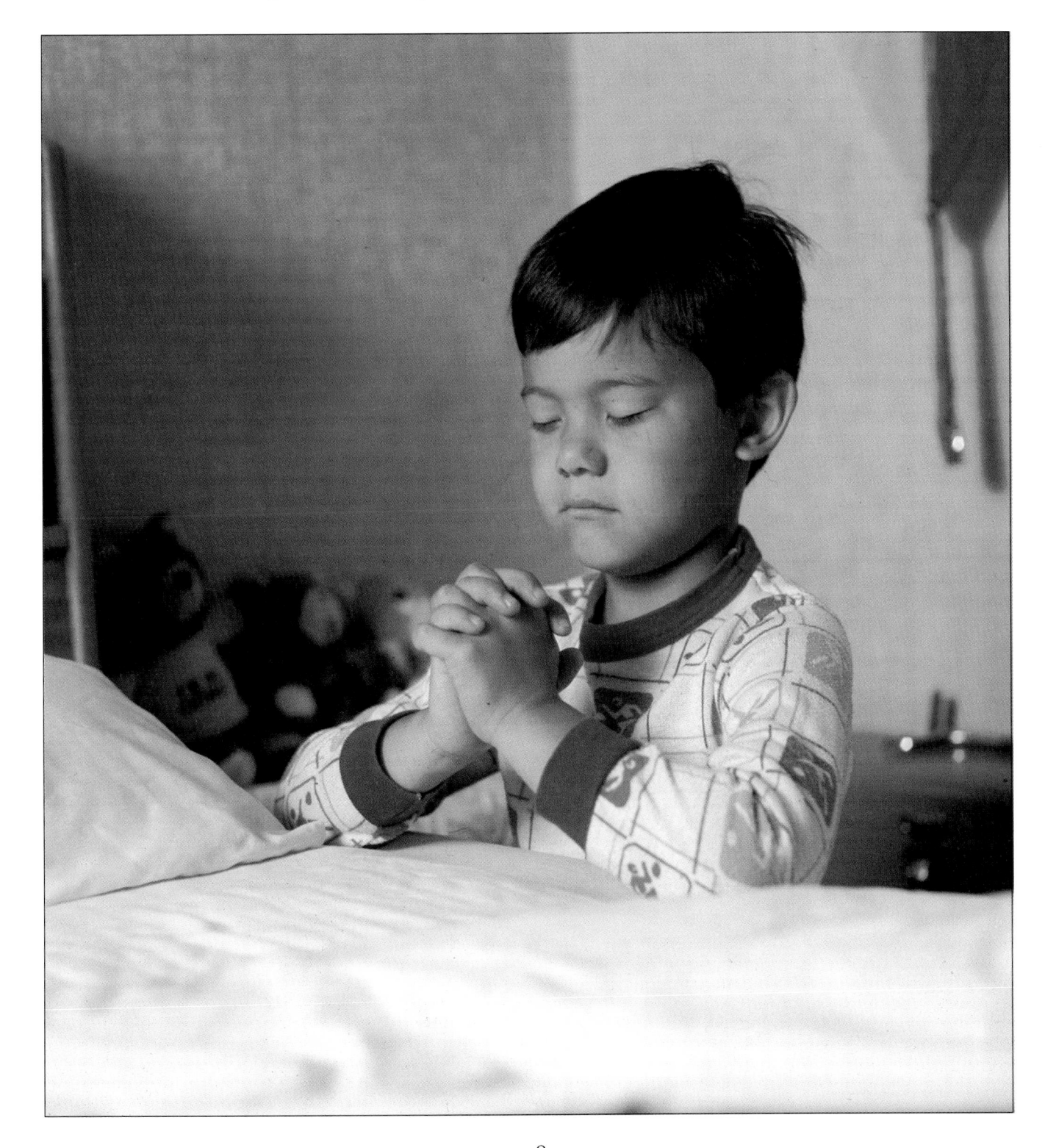

I have a talent that no one knows about but me and God. Other people may be able to do things that everyone can see, but my talent is quiet and personal.

Each night, before I go to sleep, I kneel beside my bed and pray. I talk to God like He's my friend, because that's exactly what He is.

I ask Him to watch out for all the people in the world. I thank Him for giving me a warm bed to sleep in and good food to eat.

Then I tell Him about my friends—about how Peter's mom and dad fight all the time, about how Karen's sister is sick, about how the new boy in school needs more friends, and about how I saw Mrs. Lawson, my teacher, crying the other day.

I ask Him to show me what to do so I can help my friends be happy. I ask Him to help me be kind to the new boy in school who says he doesn't like me. Then, before I'm finished, I pray for a good night's sleep so I can study hard the next day.

I figure God already knows about the problems my friends are having. But I want to make sure He knows I know about them; then we can work on them together.

Prayer is just a quiet talent, but I think it's important. Sometimes I notice that my friends seem a little happier after I've talked to God about their problems. That makes me feel good inside.

Use Your Talent—Watch It Grow

Make a prayer list. List anything you're troubled about. When you kneel to pray, have the list in front of you and talk to God about each thing you've written. This way, you won't forget anyone or anything important.

Write and then memorize a couple of prayers to say in public. The next time someone asks you to pray, you're ready! Remember to include lots of "thank-yous" and praises in your prayers. People need to be reminded of how much God has done for them.

Make a Book of Remembrances (Memories) just like the children of Israel did. In this book, write down all the things Jesus has done for you, like helping you get well or protecting you on a long journey. Then, when you pray, you'll have a list of "thank-yous" for God.

Being Kind Makes Me Happy

God has given everyone special talents. My talent is kindness.

Being kind means that if you see someone having a problem, you want to help.

When my friend Erin got sick last week, I picked some bright flowers in the field by my house and gave them to her. She said they were pretty.

Yesterday, a new girl came to our school. The other kids made fun of her and laughed at her red hair. I didn't laugh. At lunchtime, I sat with her so she wouldn't be lonely. My mom says that's what kindness is.

Using your kindness talent means helping animals too. I always make sure our cat has food to eat and water to drink. I play gently with her and *never* pull her tail. She just purrs and purrs. Kindness makes both animals and people happy.

My mom says Jesus was always using His kindness talent. He listened to people tell about their troubles and helped them whenever they asked Him to.

Jesus never was unkind. Even when people hurt Him, He just prayed and asked God the Father to forgive them.

Kindness is a talent everyone who loves God can have. When you're kind, you're doing what Jesus would do.

Use Your Talent—Watch It Grow

Start your own Kindness Patrol. Keep your eyes open for people who need someone to be kind to them. It may be a boy or girl who's sad or lonely. It could be an adult who has lots of worries. When you see someone who needs kindness, stop what you're doing and try to help and encourage them.

Make a colorful bookmark for your Bible. On it, print these words: " 'Be kind and loving to each other.' Ephesians 4:32" (International Children's Bible). Then every time you open your Bible, it will remind you that Jesus wants us to be kind. Make "kindness" bookmarks for your friends too.

Write a letter to someone who is sick and has to miss school or church. Tell him that you're sad he's sick and hope he gets well soon. If possible, ask your mom or dad to take you to that person's house for a quick visit.

I Understand Directions

Last Friday my mom asked me to help her clean the house. "Here's what I need you to do," she said. "First, take out the garbage and put new plastic bags in the trash cans. Then sweep the front walk, feed the dog, and find your sister's yellow socks."

"No problem," I replied. In a flash I was out the door, garbage bag in hand. Twenty minutes later I went to find Mom.

"Are you done already?" she said, looking around the room. The garbage was gone, new plastic bags lined the trash cans, the front walk didn't have a speck of dirt on it, my sister's yellow socks hung by the washing machine, and our dog Samson was just finishing his supper.

"You did all the things I told you to do," my mom said proudly. "You have a wonderful talent."

"I do?"

"Yes. You understand directions. You remembered everything. That's a very good talent to have. With a talent like that, you will be a good worker for Jesus. He has given us directions on how to live a happy life. Understanding and following those directions are very important."

"Thanks, Mom," I said. "If you need my talent any more, just ask."

"Well, as a matter of fact, there are a couple more things you can do for me. Wash your face, put on a clean shirt, get in the car, and we'll go get some frozen yogurt for dessert to go with dinner."

Sometimes understanding directions is a lot of fun!

I Make Joyful Music

Jesus gave me a wonderful talent. Now you may not think it's so wonderful when you hear it, but don't worry—my dad says some things get better with time and lots of practice.

My talent is making music. No, I can't play the organ like the woman at church or sing songs like the choir leader. My music is simple, quiet.

When I'm all alone, playing in my room, I sing to myself. I think about the songs I hear at church and sing them to my cat, my goldfish, and my favorite doll.

For my birthday, Dad gave me a little keyboard. It doesn't have a lot of notes on it, but it's fun to play. I press one key at a time and listen to the sound. I try to sing along.

Playing my little keyboard and singing songs makes me feel happy inside. When I make music, I pretend I hear violins and trumpets playing along with me. I imagine choirs singing and beautiful organ melodies echoing all around.

Sometimes when I'm singing to myself, my mom will say, "That's a lovely song. Will you sing it to me too?" I stand straight and tall and try to make every note as pretty as possible. My mom always says, "Jesus gave you a wonderful talent. Remember to use it to bring joy to other people." I smile. It won't be hard to do that because making music brings joy to me.

13

I Like to Talk

...talent. I don't mean silly ... talking or just making ... . I mean the kind of talk- ... u teach someone some- ... know before.

...My dad says I could talk ...e water. I've never tried ...

...e afraid to get up in front ... say something. Not me. ...cher asks if there's some- one who would like to read out loud from a book, I raise my hand fast!

When I talk, I speak carefully, not going too fast or too slowly. I want everyone to understand what I'm saying.

My teacher says I can use my talent for Jesus when I grow up. She says I could be a preacher, teacher, businessman, or maybe a lawyer. All these people have to do a lot of talking.

The best kind of talking is when you say things that will help people. Jesus liked to talk. He told stories, spoke about heaven, read out loud from the Bible, and explained many important things to the people who wanted to listen.

Whenever Jesus talked, people listened, because He told them things they needed to hear. That's what I want to do. I want to say important things people need to hear.

Do you think you have this talent too? Come visit me. We'll talk about it.

Use Your Talent—Watch It Grow

Start a speech club where everyone who joins can write and give a speech to the rest. You can talk about school, your last family vacation, your favorite pet. Encourage each member to speak slowly and clearly. Clap loudly when each speech is over.

Learn a nice poem or interesting story and ask your mom or dad to take you to visit a retirement home. The people there would love to hear you speak. At Christmastime, learn a special holiday poem and share it with your friends.

Think about a miracle God performed for you and then ask your pastor if you can share it with the adults during church time. At the end of your speech, invite everyone to remember a miracle God performed for them.

I'm a Good Leader

God has given every boy and girl at least one talent. Some of my friends have talents I don't have, and I have a couple they don't have. Because no one on earth has *every* talent, we all need to work together.

When a group wants to get something done, they choose a good leader to keep the project organized. That's my talent. I'm a good leader.

Now, don't think this is because I'm extra smart or anything like that. I make mistakes. But a good leader knows mistakes are a way to learn things.

When the teacher asked my class to make a geography poster at school, I thought and thought about the talents my classmates have, and then I suggested who should do what. I said, "Tony, you can draw well, so will you paint the picture of South America? Jennifer, you write words very nicely, so will you print the country names? And, Jason, you're the tallest; will you please hang the poster on the wall?"

Then I held the paint jar for Tony, made sure Jennifer had room to work, and found a hammer and nail for Jason. Together, we got the job done. Good leaders don't do everything all by themselves. They need the talents of other people to do things. They thank everyone who helped out.

Jesus, the world's greatest leader, needs our talents so He can tell people how much He loves them. Will you help? I'll show you how. That's what good leaders do best.

Use Your Talent—Watch It Grow

 The next time you're put in charge of something, make a list of everyone who helps you. After the project is finished, write a thank-you note to each helper. Let them know how much you appreciate their hard work.

A good leader looks for ways to get things done better. Study the activities at your school and write down some suggestions to share with your teacher. Maybe the trash should be collected more often, or the halls need to be swept twice a day. Make sure you include some good ideas on how to make your suggestions work.

 Take charge of a cleanup on your block. Ask friends and neighbors to help pick up papers and bottles along the street. Call a local newspaper reporter and tell him or her what your group is planning to do. Maybe you'll see everyone's picture in the morning paper!

I'm a Good Follower

I'm a shy person. I get embarrassed a lot. Whenever my teacher asks me to do something up in front, it makes me a little scared inside.

Some of my classmates feel the same way I do. But we don't talk about it much.

The other day, I found out something neat about myself. I found out I have a talent, an important talent. Was I surprised!

One of the sixth-graders named Lisa was building a fort. She needed someone to get some branches for the walls, so she said, "Hey, Shawn, will you please bring me those branches over there and help me build this wall?"

I said, "Sure!"

Soon we had a great fort built. Lisa said, "Shawn, thank you for helping me. You did everything like I asked you to. I thought you were just a shy person, but now I think you're a good follower."

She was right. I was a good follower! I worked hard doing what I was told to do, didn't complain or fuss, and had a good time.

Later that day, during worship, my dad read a story about Jesus and His disciples. It told how the disciples helped Jesus do His work of healing people and preaching in the villages. They learned how to be good followers too.

I'm still a shy person. But I know something about myself that makes me feel happy. When something needs to be done, I'll help any way I can.

This is one talent I'm going to use all my life.

I Am Enthusiastic

Life can be hard for a kid. Home may not be as fun as you'd like it to be, friends may turn their noses up at you, the teacher may give you too many assignments, and your dog may bite your toe. Yes, life can sometimes be a real drag.

That's when you need a very special talent from God. And He's happy to let you use it. That talent is enthusiasm.

I use my enthusiasm talent every day. When something happens to me that makes me mad, sad, hurt, or troubled, my enthusiasm kicks in. Like yesterday. My friend Terry decided to stop speaking to me. Well, OK. I went to the library and found a neat book on space travel and enjoyed the silence (Terry talks a lot when he does talk). I got so enthusiastic about the book, I showed it to Peter. We had a good time looking at the pictures.

Last week, my mom and dad had a big argument. I hate it when they do that. Well, OK. I waited until they were finished and then told them both how much I loved them and how much I enjoyed living with them between fights. They looked at each other and started laughing.

Enthusiasm means finding good things right in the middle of bad things.

My grandma says I have "positive thinking." She says Jesus created enthusiasm so we could survive living in a sinful world.

Someday, we will all live in heaven. I like to think about that. It will be fun to be enthusiastic for ever and ever.

19

I Appreciate People

"What's the matter with you?" my dad asked the other day.

I said quietly, "I don't have a single talent. All the other kids at school have at least one, but I don't. It's making me feel sad."

My dad sat down beside me. "God has given everyone a talent or two."

"He must have given mine to someone else. Take Wilton, for instance. He can sing and play the piano all at the same time. It's amazing. I like to sit and listen to him.

"And Jessica, she can add numbers almost as fast as you can say them. I can say four numbers and zap, she has them all added up. I told her she should be a schoolteacher or a scientist.

"And Michael, he paints pictures that look almost real. He gave me a picture of a horse jumping over a fence. I stuck it on my desk so I could see it every day. He's always giving me pictures."

Dad began to smile. Then he started to laugh.

"Don't make fun of me," I said, feeling a little hurt. "I can't help it if I don't have a talent."

"But you do," Dad said, putting his arms around me. "All these other kids like to show you *their* talents because you appreciate them, and you tell them so. It makes them feel happy."

I began to smile. "Appreciating other people's talents is a talent?"

"Of course it is. Jesus said we should be kind and loving. Appreciating others is a wonderful way of doing that."

Then I began to laugh too. "I guess I'd better start appreciating my own talent, now that I know I have one." And I do.

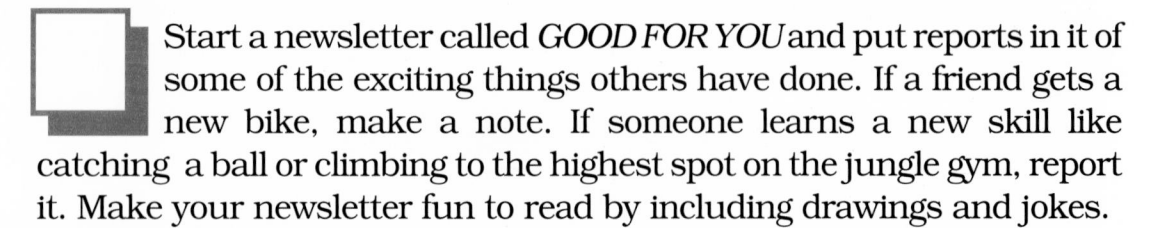

Use Your Talent—Watch It Grow

When a friend or classmate does something neat, like getting an A on a quiz or painting an interesting picture, write him a note, saying how much you appreciate his talent.

Start a newsletter called *GOOD FOR YOU* and put reports in it of some of the exciting things others have done. If a friend gets a new bike, make a note. If someone learns a new skill like catching a ball or climbing to the highest spot on the jungle gym, report it. Make your newsletter fun to read by including drawings and jokes.

Hold a press conference to announce when a friend or classmate does something super, such as finishing a hard project or getting some type of award. Have everyone clap.

I'm Learning to Manage Money

Money doesn't grow on trees. I know. I've checked. But I do know where money comes from. Hard work.

Earning money is good. Being careful how you spend it is just as important too. It's called managing money. That's my talent.

Many of my friends earn an allowance or do jobs for neighbors. That's great. But then they spend the money as fast as they earn it. That's not so great. When something really special comes along, like a sale on bicycles, they don't have enough money to buy one.

I manage my money by putting it in my bank account right away. I keep careful records of my dollars and cents so I know how much I've saved. And if I see something I want to buy, I don't ask myself, "Do I need that?" Instead I ask, "Can I possibly do without it?" I save lots of money that way.

There's another thing I do with my money when I earn it. I pay God one penny for every ten I earn. This is called returning the tithe to God. The Bible says we should do it. My mom and dad agree. Returning tithe and giving offerings are ways of asking Jesus to help you manage your money. When you put your tithe envelope in the offering plate at church, you're saying to Jesus, "Thank You for helping me earn my money. Now please help me spend the rest of it the best way I should."

The other day my mom was sick. I went to the store and bought her some pretty flowers with my own money. It made me very happy to do that. My mom put the flowers in a vase right beside her bed so she could look at them. I think the best thing about managing money is using it to make other people happy.

Use Your Talent—Watch It Grow

Collect a small supply of tithe and offering envelopes at church and place them in your dresser. Then, when you have figured out your earnings for the week, put your tithe and offerings in the envelope and take it to church. You might need Mom or Dad to help you at first, but soon you'll be returning tithe and giving offerings to God all by yourself.

Ask your mom or dad to help you open a savings account in your name at the bank. Then carefully save part of your allowance or odd-job money each week. Keep careful records of how many dollars you put into the account.

I Like Being Neat and Clean

24

Jesus gives everyone at least one talent. Would you like to know what mine is?

A few months ago, my dad said to me, "I think you have a special talent. You always make sure your room is straightened up—all your toys are put away, and your bed is made. And I notice that you wash your hands before *every* meal. God has given you the talent of being neat and clean."

I'd never heard of a neat-and-clean talent before, but my dad is pretty smart. He should know a talent when he sees one.

Since he told me that, I've watched myself very carefully, and you know, he's right. I like to see things where they're supposed to be. I like for my face and hands to be clean (except when I'm playing trucks with my friend Debbie).

My dad said having a neat-and-clean talent will help me all my life, no matter what kind of work I do when I grow up.

He says being neat and clean helps fight sickness, makes people enjoy being around you, and makes Jesus happy too.

Jesus was always neat and clean. He took special care of the things that belonged to Him. He wants us to do the same with our toys, books, beds, and bodies. By using our neat-and-clean talent, we're saying Thank You to God for what He's given us.

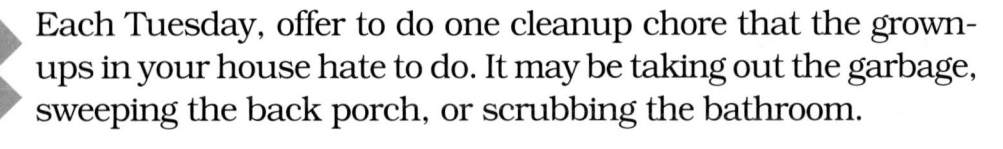

Use Your Talent—Watch It Grow

Each Tuesday, offer to do one cleanup chore that the grown-ups in your house hate to do. It may be taking out the garbage, sweeping the back porch, or scrubbing the bathroom.

If you have a brother or sister who doesn't like cleaning up their bedroom, offer to do it yourself in trade for something you don't like doing. Maybe they could fix your bike or help you with a school assignment you don't understand. Write down your agreements.

Offer to help an elderly neighbor keep his or her house and yard clean. If she accepts your offer, tell her you'll do it under one condition—that she tell you exciting stories from when she was a child. This will make the job more fun for both of you.

I Help Stop Fights

My friend Jimmy got into a fight the other day. Kirsten said he was a crybaby, and Jimmy said he was *not*. Kirsten said he was. Jimmy said he was not. Kirsten said . . . well, you get the picture.

All at once, Kirsten reached out and pushed poor Jimmy to the ground. There was yelling and punching and all sorts of stuff going on.

I don't like to see my friends fighting, so I tried to stop it. Let me tell you right now that stopping a fight can be painful. I hurt my arm and my ear, but they did stop fighting.

I asked Kirsten why he called Jimmy a crybaby. Kirsten said it was because Jimmy had gotten in front of him at the drinking fountain. I know this doesn't make sense, but most fights don't.

Jimmy said he didn't know Kirsten was waiting in line because he was just standing there talking with Alice Thompson, the fifth-grader. Jimmy said he was very thirsty and wanted to get a drink right then!

After Jimmy and Kirsten talked about what had happened, they both agreed that they shouldn't have been fighting. They each said they were sorry and went out to play kickball. I went to get an ice bag for my ear.

My teacher says I have a God-given talent. She says I'm a peacemaker, that I can help my classmates stop fighting with each other. She said Jesus was a peacemaker too. Well, if I can be like Jesus, then that's what I want to be, even if it is hard on ears.

26

Cooking for Health

Everybody likes to eat. But not everybody is careful about *what* they eat. They just buy food because it tastes good or comes in a pretty package. Then they wonder why they get sick so much.

I learned in school that eating fresh fruits and vegetables, beans, and grains instead of a lot of meat, candy, or food packed with chemicals can actually make you feel better. That made sense to me because God created fruits, vegetables, beans, and grains for us to eat. He certainly would know what we needed to stay healthy.

So, my dad said he would grow a garden if I learned to cook. Mom said she would help too. That's how I got my talent. I call it my "Cooking for Health" talent. It's fun.

As the big garden was growing in our backyard, I collected recipes from friends, neighbors, and magazines. The library had a whole bunch of books on cooking "naturally."

Then, when the vegetables were ready, my mom and I worked and worked until we could make delicious dinner dishes from carrots, squash, potatoes, tomatoes, onions, corn, and cucumbers. We seasoned everything just right so their natural flavors would tickle the tongue. Dad was impressed.

Now, whenever I cook something, I ask myself two questions—is this food healthy, and what can I do to make it taste great?

Even if you can't grow a garden at your house, you can ask your mom or dad to buy fresh fruits and vegetables and other healthy food at the store. Then, you can have a Cooking for Health talent too. You will feel good!

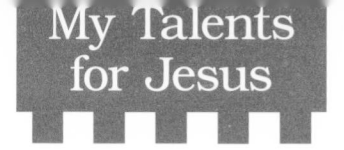

I Have Helpful Hands

Jesus gave me a very important talent. It's my helpful hands.

Whenever my dad asks me to take out the trash, my helpful hands get busy and do it right away.

When my mom asks me to clean up my room, my helpful hands pick up my racing cars, socks, bathing suit, books, hairbrush, football, rock collection, tennis shoes, and crayons.

My dad always comes to my bedroom door after I'm finished and says, "Who lives here?"

My helpful hands do a lot of other things too.

They feed our dog Matilda, dry the dishes, find lost stuff under the couch for my dad, and make sure my toys aren't where someone can trip over them. My helpful hands can stay very busy all day long.

Mom says my talent is very important. She says Jesus had helpful hands too. She says He was always busy making sure people were safe and happy, and if there was a job to do, He did it without complaining.

Do you like to help people? Maybe you have helpful hands too. The next time your mom or dad asks you to do something for them, put your hands to work. If you need any help, let me know.

Use Your Talent—Watch It Grow

Make a poster with flowers and trees on it that says, " '*Whatever work you do, do your best.*' Ecclesiastes 9:10" (ICB). Put the poster on your bedroom wall where you can see it every day.

During evening worship, have each family member write down on a small slip of paper a task they would like someone to do. Place the papers in a box, then pass it around. Let each person pick up one of the slips. (If you get your own, select again.) Then during the next few days, do the task written on the slip. This gets everyone's helpful hands busy.

Try to find one person each day who needs your help. Walk up and say, "May I help you do that?" Then do your very best.

God Gives Everybody Time

There's a special talent Jesus gives everybody. You have it, your mom and dad have it, the man who sells fruit at the corner market has it, all the people driving by in their cars have it too.

This talent is time.

Jesus gives everybody twenty-four hours every day. It's a wonderful talent to have. You can use your time to work, study, play, sleep, eat, talk to your friends, go on a trip, look at a picture book, help out at home, even write a poem.

Jesus wants us to use our time talent carefully. He wants us to make sure we don't waste the hours and minutes He's given us.

If we just sit and watch television when we could be helping someone, we're wasting our time talent. If we spend our time arguing with our friends, being selfish with our toys, or forgetting to pray to God each day, we're not using this important talent as we should.

But if we always find some time to help others or teach ourselves something new or to learn more about God and His love for us, then we are using our time talent wisely. God will smile and say, "That person is making the best of every minute of every day."

Time is precious. Ask Jesus to help you use this important talent as He would.

Use Your Talent—Watch It Grow

Write down your plans for tomorrow on a piece of paper and put it on your dresser. The next morning, review what you want to do during the day. This will keep you from forgetting anything important. Using time wisely helps get everything done.

Just for fun, keep track of how much time you spend doing what you do during the day. This will include time for school, play, eating, studying, worship, and so on. After you've done this for three days, look at your list and ask yourself, "Do I spend enough time thinking about Jesus and doing what He wants me to do?"

Set aside thirty minutes each day to read or watch a video on religious subjects. It may be a music video or a picture book about the Bible. Always remember to include time for Jesus in your busy day.